A New Day

Poems

Jean Goulbourne

Worlds of Possibility LLC

https://www.juliarios.com/worlds-of-possibility/

Copyright © 2023 Jean Goulbourne

A New Day
Jean Goulbourne

Paperback ISBN: 978-1-961778-02-3

Ebook ISBN: 978-1-961778-03-0

Cover and interior design by Julia Rios

Contents

Part One

I rejoice

Arrival

There is a shrill bird-note
In the sky
As though it portends
Better things

The day has just
Arrived
Travelling like a king

I stretch arms
Above my head
With a yawn
Like a cat

Then I smile as I see
The light of day
Glee –filled
With glad sun's ray

A new day

Like the tiny bird breaking
Its shell
new day dawns
Dark disappears
Green leaves glitter
With the dew
And wind
Like a morning sheet
Spreads itself

Birdsong wakes the morning
Gleeful and wild
And over the blue tent of day
Sun hovers
With a smile

Daylight

Last night the clouds were dim
And the sky dull
With dying
Even the stars seem to wilt
in the growing night

then dawn arrived
and the sun ripped
the festering flesh away
and brought the leaves
their glistening light

under the trees
the grass quit sings

glowing day is like a baby
suckling sun's ray

The epitome of bliss

A cup of coffee
In my hands

Black as skin

Heavenly smells
With morning smiles

As I linger
Over a sip

I draw a breath
Of thanks
And sigh

Eternal bliss

The valley day

In between the mountains
Lies the valley
The rocks are sharp
The climb is full of chasms
the rock face looks precipitous
And tough

I start to climb

The mountain top is far
But I climb

The valley looks safer
The sun is setting

I climb

The dark shines
in the valley

The sun is brighter
On the top
Still I climb
It's getting cool now

I arrive on a ledge

I climb
I pull myself up
I am there

I look down in the valley
It's dim

I look up
The sun is still on the horizon
I am jubilant

The deep lies behind me

I have left the valley day
Behind

Gloriously free

A bird song
Speaks of daybreak
And I awake
And see the peek of sun
Address the dawning
See the pyramid of clouds
Reflect sun's rays

See dew sparkle
On the grass
And I laugh
As I watch
And see this day unfold

I rejoice
With all things living
And all things dead
For they too leap
To celebrate this day
With birds and trees and me
Gloriously free

Nightmare's morning

It's the morning after the dream
And I stare at the ceiling

The bedclothes wrap me up
As though to protect me
Like Mama's arms
Taking me into her bed

But she is dead

No tears now
Just fears

The dark has escaped
Through the window

The sun is up

But the nightmare
remembers me

Picture

This is the story of an old man
Dying
The tales are told
in the wrinkles on his face
By the gentle eyes
Submissive and kind

This is the portrait of an old man
Dead

my father

Of poetry and me

It starts slow
Like a tiny stream
Etching its life out
Over rocks and silt
Like tardy water
From reluctant rain
Like the easing of pain
From a drought

There it begins
Flows, gathering strength
As it tumbles unceasing
Down a multitude of rocks
It filters fast across the lines of earth
building riverbanks
on its way to the sea

the outpouring of words
from the depths of me

galloping and singing
winding and ringing
like bells on a church steeple
like drums on a revival night
like children on a playfield
like boys in a pond
like a waterfall of rain
this blessing, these fingertips
on the computer keyboard
this movement from my bed of thorns
to hear the breeze that bellows
to ride the hurricane with words
to dip and fall with dinki mini tunes
to drink the sweet sap
of poetry

Part Two

Of race and me

Colour blind

When I learnt that I was black
And therefore to be scorned
I asked God why
But got no reply
Iron ripped my kinky hair straight
And I tried to stain my skin lily white
But the bleaching cream failed
Into blotches of uneven hue
And self-hate set in
I asked God when did I sin?
Still no news from him
Then young adult times tempered
That self hate
As afro and black power
Dimmed my false self-view
And I pulled on my bell bottom pants
And danced
Now we rise Angelou wise

Jean Goulbourne

We are tops with presidents and kings
I write my story and it is read
Better that than be colourless and dead

A song from black throats

When I hear
Amazing grace
Crooned from the throat
Of a black president
I take pride
In the resilience
Of my race

We came in ships
Hunted and abused
But we toiled on

Segregation
Did not deter us
Murder and mayhem
Could not control our rise
So we sing
And our voices ring

Jean Goulbourne

Across the centuries
On this ground
Amazing grace
How sweet the sound

August 1st

Last night I saw a ghost
He hovered
White beard
on coal black skin
He smiled

Too scared to smile
I covered myself
Till I remembered
August first

white beard
on coal black skin
saying
'We free
What a jubilee"

Drum

My brother
beats the drum

they call him
bum

from
his cage

he screams
his rage

Part Three

Of nationhood

After the drought

And after the drought
Came the rains blessings
On a parched land
Grass lay
And trees went a begging

but then the rains came
shaking hands reached out
to grasp
the elusive raindrops
which slithered to the ground
in bubbling protest
gurgling rushing water
into streams and rivers
and into my mouth
to satisfy my dry tongue

Power cut!

And darkness descends
Having clasped day in an iron grip
Night covers everything

Outside my window
Even stars seem dead

I creep under my blanket
And fall asleep

Our National Pride

Upon the cloth
The woman embroidered green black and gold
Interspaced with a multiplication sign that spoke lies
Sunlight dribbled through the open window
And as she took the black thread she cried
Her tears embroidering water
On the green grass of leaves

Fifty years

Gone

And we forget the woman under the window
Embroidering leaves to catch the sunlight
While crying tears to ease her pain

Here in this space

In this space
This island
Where mountains speak
And rivers ease into ocean deep
Where blue skies hover
And night skies proliferate
Where trees hum with bees
And wind cries humbug sighs
I close my eyes and conjure thoughts
Of escape

But then I look inside me
and remember the rushing rivers
the blue clad mountains
the fiery hurricane's hit on my roof
the trees talking with the breeze
and I know I will not leave it now

A New Day

I can never wash the dirt stains
From my feet

Out of sorrow

Axe cut tree
It bled for me

I cried
I thought the tree
Had died

Until I saw a bud
small and frail

'gainst wind and rain
It will prevail

Monster sea

You eating me
Like you eat mi husband?
You taking me
Like you swallow him?

You there drifting
On white sand beach
Like you innocent
With you waves
sipping at sand

but is you
eat mi husband
drag him in deep
to sleep with the mermaid
leaving me alone

A young man's longing

A young man longs to leave
Sunlit cane fields and rushing rivers
For the sky scrapers of a big city

He gets the visa
And he goes

Cleans the streets
Turns to drugs
Lives on the underground
And begs

The young man longs
for sunlit cane fields
and rushing rivers

longs
but is lost

Part Four

The wider world

Love on a rampage

The world spins
On lust's axle

A kiss
Is penetration

A look
An invitation

A wink
Is a yes
And a bare leg
A song

So what's new?
The conversation
Is forever

Jean Goulbourne

Sex is the rage
The only thing slowing it
Is death or old age

Drinking Water

Maybe if I shed tears
It would fill a cup
Except it would be salty waste matter
And unfit to drink

The millennium goal
For safe drinking water
Has not been met
And I think of my own dry
Water tank full of weeds.
For weeks it has not rained
I buy water and beg
The universe to hear my cry

Our earth no longer sings

Men came
And raped her

The rape of one woman
Is the rape
Of a nation

They murder children
The murder of a child
Is the mutilation
Of thousands

Now earth turns
Evil leaching life
And earth is crying for mercy

Our earth
no longer sings

Europe beware

Sunday morning church
And the pews are almost empty
The Minister drones on

Those who grace the pews
Are old and fast asleep
Grandchildren are at home
Playing video games

Europe beware
The migrants are coming

To fill your cathedrals
With songs and prayers

Aleppo

She hears the blast from the corner
It has been raining bombs for months now
She walks towards the sound unafraid
If she were to die, what then?

no one's loss!
her whole family
has been swallowed by a blast

she walks slowly and feels no fear
she longs to die
she sees the carnage
she sees the blood of little children
she hears the screams

she has no tears to block her sight
a child screams

"Help me please!"

Part Five

Soul food

Minds

Philosophers grow
And seeds flutter
On the globe

Yet many
Sit among the reeds
And watch
Them grow

And reeds
Even reeds
Grow taller
Than they

Anger

Anger
Sweeps memories away
Like dead leaves
After a storm
The good that friendship
Thrived on
Is left barren
And forlorn

Words are not mere winds
Winds blow and are gone
The sting of words
Remain
And the friendship
Is forever torn

Hate

Hate
That nauseous belch
Before the vomit
Sickens us all
And time will be
When the liquid flows
Backwards

Suffocating

Truth

Truth
Sits on Mount Olympus
Looking down

Can't you see
Asks truth
That the path
To the plain
is overgrown?

The golden sand dunes

So we've landed on a comet
And we've sped past Pluto

While here
On planet Earth
Seven billion puny men
Fight over turf
Trying to build Utopia
On sinking sand

Lost

He wears Nike shoes
Clean and crisp

On his head
The cap turned backwards

He is hip
He is Okay

But dark eyes tell
Of a dying soul

He twists his smart phone
As if to find himself
On the screen

Old eyes and a tree

The wrinkles on her face
Tell of ageing
And the lines under her eyes
Speak memories

But the sun is bright today

The grass shines green
The sky shimmers
birds
sense the stillness

old eyes lift and smile
at the yellow poui tree
light touches
its petals
in the tumult of day

Within the mind

Within the mind there is a candle
Lit with thought
It eats away the night
Dribbles wax upon batik'
Melding pattern upon pattern
Mixing shadow with relieving light

Whilst from the candle
Wisdom whittles
At the tallow
And the wick is eaten slowly
In the passing of its life

But upon the painting
Is etched the shadow
And the light
And within the framework
a memory will be
forever in our sight

How sweet the sorrow

How sweet the sorrow
That grieves the heart and enfeebles the mind
The swift day moves into deep dark evening
And just at twilight we hear the deathly hoot of owl
Summoning us to the bedside and to tears
And we weep the cleansing tears that liberate and free
That loose the strings that bind, the memories that
entomb
Then we seek sleep, sweet tasting and mellow.
We awake the morning with cocks' lusty crow
Never forgetting, always remembering
But as we grasp the light in our waiting palms
We see the dew dropped trees
And the singing grass blades
And we sing with them
Once more to face life
and our remaining days

About the Author

JEAN GOULBOURNE is a poet, short story writer, novelist, and educator from Cross Keys, Manchester, Jamaica. She worked as an educator in secondary schools and colleges, and was part of the writing team for The Butterfly Series, now known as The Blue Mahoe, a series of books for reluctant adolescent readers. She is also the author of several other books for children published by a variety of Jamaican and British publishers.

Her books for adults include the short story collection, *The Parable of the Mangoes*, available through Abeng Press, which (under the title *Caged Birds*) was runner up for the Una Mason prize in 1995, a poetry collection, *Woman Song*, and a novel, *Excavation*, both available through Peepal Tree Press.

Individually, her stories and poems have appeared in *Savacou*, *Bim*, *The New Voices*, *The Caribbean Writer*,

Nimrod, New Poets of Jamaica, The Literary Review, Focus, Pathways, Dreamrock, Facing the Sea, Caribbean Poetry, Caribbean Poetry Now, New World English, Bite In, Oxford book of Caribbean Poetry, The Daily News, The Jamaica Record, The Jamaica Herald, The Sunday Gleaner, The Sunday Observer Arts Magazine, The Children's Own, Scribbles, Metamorphosis, Caribbean Challenge and other magazines throughout the Caribbean.

Printed in the USA
CPSIA information can be obtained
at www.ICGtesting.com
CBHW040938231023
1459CB00024B/144

9 781961 778023